AF585263

AUSTRALIA'S ENDANGERED ANIMALS ...AND THEIR HABITATS

A FOCUS ON FRESHWATER ENVIRONMENTS

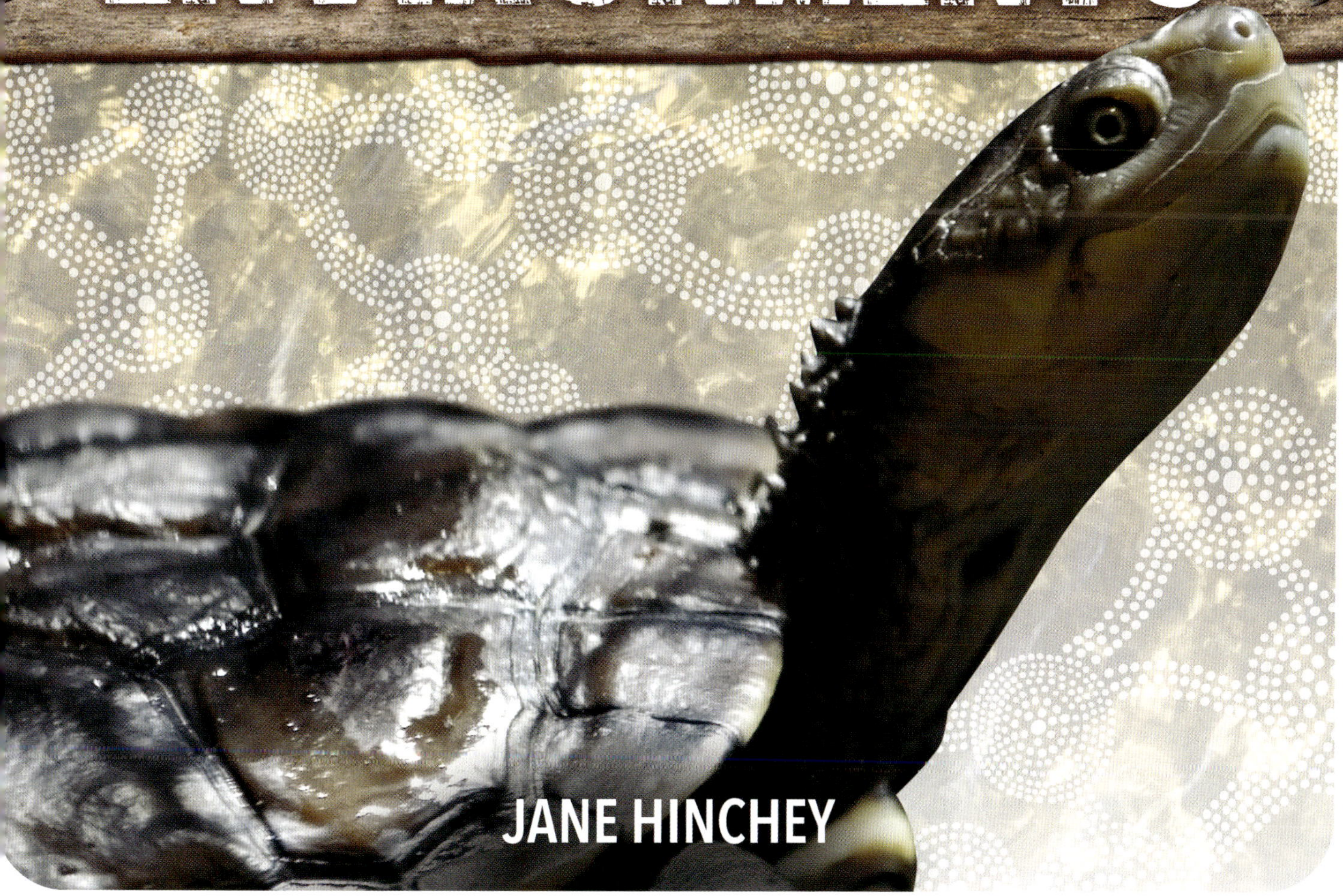

JANE HINCHEY

REDBACK publishing

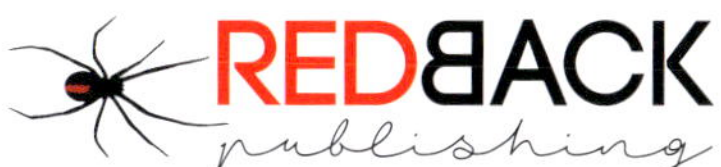

Redback Publishing
PO Box 357 Frenchs Forest NSW 2086
Australia

www.redbackpublishing.com.au
orders@redbackpublishing.com.au

ISBN 978-1-925630-78-7

Author: Jane Hinchey
Editor: Michael Anderson
Designer: Redback Publishing

Original illustrations © Redback Publishing 2019
Originated by Redback Publishing

Printed and bound in China

Acknowledgements
Abbreviations: l–left, r–right, b–bottom, t–top, c–centre, m–middle
We would like to thank the following for permission to reproduce photographs: (Images © shutterstock)
p5 by I, Beentree (Kookaburra eggs), p13tr & p15tr by Codman at English Wikipedia, p21tl By W J Bill Harrison, p21bl By Simon Fraser University - University Communications, p22bl by IgorGolovniov, p22br By Canley - Own work, CC BY-SA 4.0, p23tr by Jean-Marc Hero.

Every effort has been made to contact copyright holders of any material reproduced in this book. Any omissions will be rectified in subsequent printings if notice is given to the publisher.

A catalogue record for this book is available from the National Library of Australia

CONTENTS

Australia is unique. It is not only a country and an island, but also one of the world's seven continents. Australia was cut off from the rest of the world's landmass for over 100 million years, which allowed for a diverse range of animals to flourish. It is home to more than one million species of plants and animals, many of which are found nowhere else in the world, and less than half have been described scientifically. About 85 per cent of plants, 84 per cent of mammals, 45 per cent of birds, 88 per cent of reptiles and 94 per cent of amphibians are endemic. In Australia there are more than 378 species of mammals, 828 species of birds, 300 species of lizards, 140 species of snakes and two species of crocodiles.

FABULOUS FAUNA

Among Australia's best-known animals are the kangaroo, koala, echidna, platypus, wallaby and wombat.

AUSTRALIA ANIMAL CLASSIFICATION CHART

Scientists classify animals into groups in order to study and understand them. Each group can have numerous sub-groups. Australia's animals are divided into six major groups.

Group	Characteristics	Examples
AMPHIBIAN	Lives on both land and water Has smooth skin, webbed feet Lays eggs	Frogs such as the spotted tree frog and corroboree frog
BIRD	Hatches from eggs Has feathers and wings	Australian bustard, cassowary, kookaburra
FISH	Lives in water Hatch from soft eggs Has fins and scales	Fish such as the Eastern freshwater cod, Australian smelt and estuary perch
MAMMAL	Warm blooded Lactate to feed young Most have body hair	Koala, wombat, kangaroo, wallaby, possum
REPTILE	Hatches from eggs Lives on land Has scales	Eastern bearded dragon, eastern brown snake, freshwater crocodile
INVERTEBRATES	No backbone Many forms of locomotion	Beetles, flies, mosquitoes, snails, worms, crabs, squid and spiders such as the redback spider

DID YOU KNOW?

Aboriginal people have a multifaceted classification system for organising knowledge, which includes the animal kingdom. This system is highly complex and includes regional, cultural and spiritual influences, as well as practical considerations such as if an animal is edible and whether it is poisonous.

UNIQUE AUSTRALIAN HABITATS

Freshwater Habitats include rivers, lakes, billabongs and ponds. They support animals such as the eastern water skink, dragonfly, platypus, the Macquarie perch and yellow-spotted bell frog.

TURN TO PAGE 10 FOR MORE INFORMATION ON FRESHWATER HABITATS

Australia's **Coastal and Ocean Habitats** encompass more than just the country's long sandy beaches and offshore islands and reefs. There are also a diverse array of sub-habitats from mangroves, lakes and river estuaries, to rocky headlands and granite coastline.

About 70 per cent of mainland Australia is arid and semi-arid desert lands. These areas include grasslands, low woodlands and shrublands, sandy and rocky areas and tall shrub areas. **Arid Habitats** support animals such as the bilby, the thorny devil, the bearded dragon and Alice Springs Mouse. Over 200 bird species are recorded from Australia's deserts. Australia's desert mammals have suffered a very high extinction rate, with animals such as the lesser bilby and desert rat kangaroo gone forever.

Australia recognises over 900 wetlands for their national importance.

Wetland Habitats include arid and alpine, inland to coastal ecosystems. Forested wetlands include mangrove forests, river red gum forests and casuarina swamps. Animals such as the northern corroboree frog, Australian pelican and pig-nosed turtle live there. Australia's wetlands are vital for many migratory birds.

Tundra, Ice and Snow Habitats range from the Alpine mountains and forests of the Snowy Mountains, to Australian Antarctic Territory. Antarctic animals include sea lions and whales, krill, penguins and squid.

Australia's cities and towns are **Urban Habitats** and include areas such as parks, gardens, ports and harbours, rivers and buildings where animals like the grey headed flying fox, Eastern water skink and Australian magpie call home.

Rainforest in Australia have been divided into four broad groups: **hot dry** in the north, **hot moist** in the northeast and both **warm dry** and **cool moist** in the southeast. Australia's Wet Tropics World Heritage Area in northeastern Queensland includes both mountain ranges covered in rainforests and lowland tropical rainforests. The Daintree is home to some of the rarest and most spectacular flora and fauna in the world. It is a complex web of diverse habitats, with creatures living at all levels of the forest, from the canopy to under the forest floor. Some of the creatures found in the rainforests include the Ulysses butterfly, the Boyd's forest dragon and the endangered southern cassowary, with only 1,200 left in Australia.

Australia's **Alpine Habitats** range from grasslands to forests and support animals such as the broad-toothed rat, Kosciuszko grasshopper and the mountain pygmy-possum.

Australia's **Dry Forests and Woodlands** support animals such as the brush-tailed phascogale, squirrel glider and regent honeyeater. Dry forests are not as tall as rainforests.

WHY ARE HABITATS IMPORTANT?

A habitat is a place that provides shelter, safety, food and water for the animals that live there. The creatures and plants all do things to help keep the whole habitat healthy and in balance and rely upon each other for their survival. Animals like cockroaches eat the dead plants and recycle the nutrients back into the soil, which helps the plants to grow. Bats, birds and insects help spread seeds. Every plant and creature serves a purpose.

Australia is a large country with many different climates that has contributed to its range of habitats. These habitats extend from Antarctica to the tropics, encompassing environments as diverse as oceans and coasts, mangroves and rivers, coastal heathlands, mountain forests and rainforests, alpine meadows, woodlands and the dry grasslands of the interior. Each habitat can also include smaller habitats within it. For example, there may be a lush waterhole in a desert environment.

Australia's unique habitats are under threat from urban and agricultural development, fishing, trawling and harvesting fossil fuels. Australia's increasing rate of destruction of native vegetation - nearly 300,000 hectares per year - further endangers nearly 1,800 threatened species. Australia is amongst the world's worst countries for deforestation.

Disrupting The Freshwater Food Web

When one species is threatened the complex habitat and food web it is a part of also becomes threatened. A food chain is a sequence of which animals eat what, while the food web links all the food chains together. The food chain from Australia's freshwater habitats encompasses many species including fish, birds, mammals and insects. While a bird species might not eat algae directly, it could feed on the fish that do. When one link in the food chain or web is threatened, it puts the entire ecosystem in danger.

WILDLIFE WARRIOR

Can you name three different habitats near where you live? What animals live there?

FOCUS ON FRESHWATER HABITATS

Australia is one of the most arid countries in the world, but it still supports a rich aquatic system. Australia's freshwater habitats encompass more than just the country's rivers. There are also a diverse array of wetlands, mangroves, lakes, ponds, streams, creeks and billabongs.
Within each of these areas there are banks and the plants that grow there, logs, rock crevices and sediment that support a diverse range of plant and animal species. These species are impacted by any changing environmental conditions.

River Catchment Areas

Australia has twelve catchment divisions. This means an entire river system, which includes its source, all its tributaries and down to its mouth. The largest of these is the Murray–Darling, beginning in Queensland flowing through New South Wales and Victoria to its mouth in South Australia.

These catchment areas can include freshwater habitats as diverse as:

- Rivers
- Creeks and streams
- Waterholes, ponds and billabongs
- Lakes
- Riparian land
- Flood plains
- Wetlands

Riparian Land

Riparian land adjoins or directly influences a body of water. It includes riverbanks, the land around creeks, lakes, ponds and wetlands. Riparian land plays an important role in freshwater ecosystems. It stabilises riverbanks, assists soil and water quality and provides animals with an array of habitats.

HABITAT DEGRADATION

There are many ways in which habitat loss can impact the animals that live there.

- Habitat loss can wipe out all the species that live in one area.
- Habitat fragmentation makes it difficult for animals to move from one area to another, as they normally would.
- Habitat alteration, such as the loss of understorey shrubs, logs, food plants, and old trees with hollows means that animals don't have protection, feeding and nesting areas.

Wetlands

Australia recognises over 900 wetlands for their national importance. They are overseen by the Australian Government, different organisations and also landowners. Specific roles and responsibilities for managing the wetlands are outlined in the Ramsar Convention, an intergovernmental treaty for the conservation of wetlands that recognises 65 wetlands in Australia.

Wetland habitats include arid and alpine, inland to coastal ecosystems. Forested wetlands include mangrove forests, river red gum forests and casuarina swamps. Wetlands are essential breeding and nursery areas for many native fish, crustaceans and waterbirds. Australia's wetlands are home to more than 200 species of freshwater fish, many of which are now threatened species. Animals such as the northern corroboree frog, Australian pelican and pig-nosed turtle live there. Australia's wetlands are vital for many migratory birds.

DID YOU KNOW?

According to the United Nations, *'The declining state of the world's freshwater resources, in terms of quantity and quality, may prove to be the dominant issue on the environment and development agenda of the coming century'*.

THE MURRAY-DARLING BASIN

The Murray–Darling Basin is Australia's largest river system, covering over a million square kilometres in southeastern Australia, or 14 per cent of the country's landmass. Its diverse landscapes and complex ecosystems include over 30,000 wetlands and 77,000 kilometres of rivers. It includes not only the Murray River and Darling River, but also many other rivers, creeks, lakes and waterways.

Animals Under Threat

The habitats of the Murray–Darling Basin are home to at least 46 species of native fish, 53 species of frog and 124 families of macroinvertebrates.

Many animals are now endangered, including 35 bird species, 5 species of snake and 16 species of mammals. 20 species of mammal from the area have already become extinct since European settlement.

Swift Parrots

Swift parrots are one of Australia's most endangered birds. They are a colourful, medium-sized parrot with a green body, dark blue crown and crimson throat and a long pointed purple-red tail. They have been severely impacted by the clearing of the forests and woodlands where they live, including the woodlands along the Murray.

MAIN THREATS

Threats to native animals in the Murray–Darling Basin include:

- Changes to the water flow and aquatic environment
- Unsustainable management practices
- Habitat fragmentation makes it difficult for animals to move from one patch to another
- Habitat alteration such as the loss of understorey shrubs, logs, food plants and old trees with hollows
- Habitat loss and degradation
- Invasive species

FAST FACT

40 per cent of the food grown in Australia comes from the Murray-Darling Basin.

MURRAY COD

IUCN STATUS: Critically Endangered

ENVIRONMENTAL PROTECTION OF BIODIVERSITY AND CONSERVATION ACT: Vulnerable

The Murray cod is Australia's largest native freshwater fish. The cod has a cream to white belly and green mottled pattern on the body and head. It has a large mouth and rounded tail. It's a long-lived fish and one cod was aged at 48 years. It is carnivorous, feeding on other fish.

Numbers in the Murray River have severely depleted. Commercial overfishing in the late 1800s severely depleted the Murray cod population. While this commercial fishing is now banned, recreational overfishing is still an issue. Small numbers are present in the Nepean River and Yarra River, but they have failed to establish in other rivers where they have been selectively stocked. Other threats include loss of and changes to habitats, dams and river blackwater events that cause the cod to suffocate.

In 2010, a Murray Cod Recovery Program was prepared. The aim is to expand the cod population to 60 per cent of pre-European settlement numbers by 2060.

A MIGHTY COD

The largest recorded Murray cod was 1.8m long and weighed 113kg!

Aboriginal Culture

The Murray cod plays an important role in Aboriginal culture. Stories tell of a huge Murray cod forming the Murray River.

AUSTRALIA'S FRESHWATER ANIMALS

Australia is one of the most arid countries in the world, but it still supports a rich aquatic system. Australia's freshwater habitats encompass more than just the country's rivers. There are also a diverse array of wetlands, mangroves, lakes, ponds, streams, creeks and billabongs. Each of these areas supports a diverse range of plant and animal species, which are impacted by any changing environmental conditions.

Many animals rely on freshwater habitats for survival. If these animals and their habitats are not protected, they are at risk of becoming extinct. Other species that rely on these environments are classified as vulnerable, which means they are close to becoming endangered.

Some threatened animals of Australia's freshwater habitats are:

- Western swamp tortoise
- Southern purple-spotted gudgeon
- Green and golden bell frog
- Magpie goose
- Baw Baw frog
- Mary River cod
- Murray River cod
- False rat
- Lungfish
- Pedder Galaxias
- Freckled duck

THE GIANT DRAGONFLY ENDANGERED IN NSW

Found in swamps and bogs along the east coast of NSW, the endangered Giant Dragonfly's name is deceiving. It is actually only the second largest dragon fly in Australia. They eat insects and spiders and are at risk from pollution, fertilisers and chemicals, invasive weeds and cats.

CLASSIFICATION AND IDENTIFICATION

When identifying characteristics that make a species vulnerable, the international classification system used is overseen by the International Union for the Conservation of Nature (IUCN) red list.

There are many ways to classify species. We can choose any characteristic as a basis for sorting animals. These may include body form, colour pattern, mode of development or genetics. Classification helps organise the differences within and between groups of animals. Classification of animals helps identify them, understand them, quantify the threat to them and take steps to conserve a species.

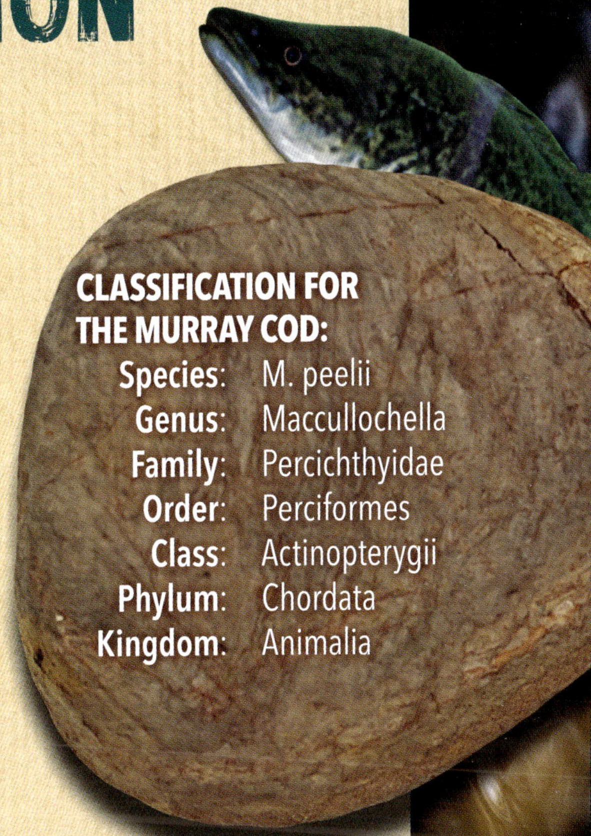

CLASSIFICATION FOR THE MURRAY COD:

Species: M. peelii
Genus: Maccullochella
Family: Percichthyidae
Order: Perciformes
Class: Actinopterygii
Phylum: Chordata
Kingdom: Animalia

CAN YOU COMPLETE THE CLASSIFICATION CHART BELOW?

ANIMAL	LISTED AS	FOOD	SHELTER	THREATS
MURRAY COD				
SOUTHERN CORROBOREE FROG				
NORTHERN CORROBOREE FROG				
SWIFT PARROT				
PLATYPUS				

ISSUES AFFECTING FRESHWATER ENVIRONMENTS

Australia's freshwater environments have been impacted by human development such as farms and industry. Farms use river water to irrigate crops. Dams have been built and river water diverted. Rivers, lakes and other water systems have been inundated with toxic chemicals from farms and factories. Wetlands are among the most modified and damaged ecosystems in the country, with many being filled in for land development. As a result, Australia's freshwater habitats have changed enormously and the species that live there have been severely impacted.

Habitat Destruction

Australia's population increase has brought huge changes to Australia's coastal habitats. Habitats have been cleared for houses, thousands of kilometres of roads, for farms and ports. Farming, logging and timber plantations, aquaculture and land clearing pose major threats to the environment and threaten between 60 and 70 per cent of the species in the area exploited.

Climate Change

Climate change is affecting, and will continue to affect, freshwater habitats in numerous ways including directly altered weather and rainfall patterns. These events could disrupt the normal cycle of variability to which animals and plants have adapted. Freshwater species are vulnerable to even the slightest rise in water temperature because they are usually limited in their habitat options. Severe weather events such as drought, floods and fire also impact these environments, and climate change effects their frequency and intensity.

Changing Ecosystems

An animal's survival often depends on the animal's ecosystem maintaining balance. Any change to the ecosystem can impact the species living there. One example of this is the food chain. The loss of the smallest creature can impact the larger creatures that feed off them, all the way to the top of the food chain. These interconnected food webs are an essential part of the overall ecosystem.

FERAL CATS

Since the British arrived in 1788, about 11 per cent of Australia's 273 native mammals have gone extinct, with a major factor being the introduction of cats. The threat of feral cats to Australia's native species is greater than that of any other predator and substantially more of a threat than the loss of habitat. It's estimated that feral cats eat 75 million native animals a night - more than 20 billion mammals, reptiles, birds and even insects every year.

OVERFISHING

Australia's freshwater rivers and wetlands are some of the most diverse in the world. From the 1860s, a large inland commercial fishery developed, based mainly on the Murray and Murrumbidgee rivers and fish such as the Murray cod began to decline.

All four freshwater cod species have been overfished and are now listed as threatened or endangered:

- Murray cod
- Trout cod
- Eastern freshwater cod
- Mary River cod

AMAZING ALGAE

Algae play a critical role in freshwater habitats. They produce about half the oxygen in Earth's atmosphere and are a major source of food for aquatic animals. There are thought to be at least 12,000 types of marine and freshwater algae species in Australia. While algae is necessary for aquatic environments, sometimes these environments are impacted by harmful algae blooms. This excessive growth of certain types of algae can be harmful to the environment and the animals that live there.

FAST FACT

The primary factors causing this loss of wildlife include:

- Feral foxes, pigs, goats, rabbits, donkeys, horses, camels, buffalo and feral cattle
- Changes in fire regimes, especially an increase in the extent and severity of wildfires
- Clearing native vegetation
- Weeds
- Hunting
- Factory and industrial waste

ANIMALS IN DANGER

Australia has the worst mammal extinction rate in the world. Globally, one out of three mammal extinctions in the last 400 years has occurred in Australia. Furthermore, over 1,700 plant and animal species are listed as threatened with extinction.

The International Union for Conservation of Nature

Many factors are used to assess the conservation status of a species. The International Union for Conservation of Nature is the global authority on the status of the natural world and the actions needed to protect it. The IUCN gathers data about different species from a huge range of sources, such as biologists, conservationists and statisticians. The IUCN Red List of Threatened Species is recognised globally as the authority on the status of endangered animals. It divides species into nine different categories:

- Extinct (EX)
- Extinct in the Wild (EW)
- Critically Endangered (CR)
- Endangered (EN)
- Vulnerable (VU)
- Near Threatened (NT)
- Least Concern (LC)
- Data Deficient (DD)
- Not Evaluated (NE)

Species in the Critically Endangered, Endangered and Vulnerable categories are all considered 'threatened.'

Extinct Animals

Extinction is when every single member of a species dies and none are left alive. Scientists go to great lengths to determine that a species is extinct – a process that begins with careful monitoring of the species while it still exists.

Since European settlement, 24 birds, 7 frogs and 27 mammal species or subspecies have become extinct in Australia. This list includes:

- thylacine, Tasmanian tiger
- bulldog rat
- dusky flying fox
- desert bandicoot
- crescent nail-tail wallaby
- blue-grey mouse
- long-tailed hopping mouse
- toolache wallaby
- eastern hare wallaby
- gastric brooding frog
- Lord Howe Island thrush
- paradise parrot
- Tasmanian emu

TASMANIAN TIGER

In Australia, animals are classified at both State and Federal levels. At Federal level the current categories are:

STATUS	NUMBER OF SPECIES THREATENED	ANIMALS INCLUDE
EXTINCT	Frogs (4) Birds (22) Mammals (27) Other animals (1)	• lesser bilby • desert rat kangaroo
EXTINCT IN THE WILD	Fishes (1)	• Pedder galaxias
CRITICALLY ENDANGERED	Fishes (8) Frogs (5) Reptiles (10) Birds (16) Mammals (5) Other animals (28)	• desert mouse • grey nurse shark (east coast) • short-nosed sea snake • great knot • Leadbeater's possum
ENDANGERED	Fishes (16) Frogs (14) Reptiles (18) Birds (51) Mammals (37) Other animals (22)	• Murray hardyhead • spotted tree frog • red-tailed black cockatoo • Australian bittern • blue whale • northern quoll
VULNERABLE	Fishes (24) Frogs (10) Reptiles (33) Birds (66) Mammals (67) Other animals (11)	• great white shark • orange-bellied frog • striped legless skink • sei whale
CONSERVATION DEPENDENT	Fishes (7)	• eastern gemfish • southern bluefin tuna

TOTAL = 503

ENDANGERED SHARKS

ENDANGER SPECIE AREA

About 180 of the world's 400 species of sharks are found in Australian waters, and 70 are thought to be endemic. Sharks are mainly found in coastal habitats, however many sharks are also found in freshwater systems, such as rivers and estuaries.

A number of shark species are now listed as Threatened under the *Environmental Protection and Biodiversity Conservation Act 1999*. Sharks are extremely important in maintaining the balance in their ecosystems and a loss of shark population impacts the whole food web.

NORTHERN RIVER SHARK

STATUS: Endangered
FEATURES: A steely grey shark that can grow up to two metres in length.

ABOUT: Not much is known about this shark, however current monitoring will hopefully change that.

HABITAT: Also known as the New Guinea river shark, the northern river shark lives in the tidal rivers of Australia and New Guinea. At present it is known to occur in only ten locations, and lives in brackish, primarily estuarine locations rather than solely freshwater.

MAIN THREATS: Small numbers and limited habitats make the northern river shark vulnerable to habitat degradation and commercial and recreational fishing activities.

NUMBERS: A survey in 2002 estimated the population to be around 250 mature individuals.

FAST FACT: Deliberate capture of northern river sharks is illegal in the Northern Territory.

DID YOU KNOW?
Sharks predate the dinosaurs by 200 million years.

SPEARTOOTH SHARK

STATUS: Critically Endangered

ABOUT: The speartooth shark is a species of whaler shark and is Australia's largest freshwater river fish. It has a dark grey dorsal colouration, a large second dorsal fin and narrow spear-like teeth in the lower jaw, which is where it gets its name.

MAIN THREATS: The speartooth shark is especially at risk from habitat degradation due to its preference for specific areas. The speartooth shark is also under threat from bait nets and illegal fishing.

HABITAT: The speartooth shark inhabits the eastern Gulf of Carpentaria and some rivers of Cape York Peninsula, Queensland and other low salinity and freshwater coastal marine waters, mangrove rivers and tidal reaches of large tropical rivers in northern Australia and New Guinea.

NUMBERS: About 2,500.

FUN FACT: It has very small eyes and hunts in river waters with poor visibility, so has adapted to hunt in darkness.

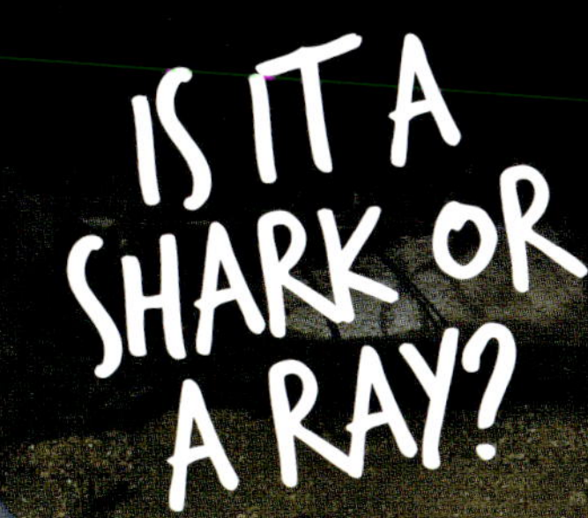

Largetooth Sawfish

The largetooth sawfish looks like a shark, but is actually a ray. It has a long snout, or saw, with 14 to 23 large rostral teeth used to feed on small fish, prawns and other crustaceans. It can range in colour from grey to golden brown with a cream underbelly.

While they are sometimes found in marine habitats and can tolerate a range of salinities, they are predominantly a freshwater species found in rivers across northern Australia.

Although not commercially targeted, the sawfish have been impacted by fishing. Their long snout makes them particularly susceptible to being caught in nets. They have also been impacted by habitat degradation and change.

There are five species of sawfish and all are listed as either Critically Endangered or Endangered. The largetooth sawfish, previously known as freshwater sawfish, is listed by the IUCN as Critically Endangered.

FRESHWATER FROGS

Australia has over 200 species of frog, but the populations are declining. Of these, 15 species are currently endangered, 12 are listed as vulnerable and 4 have become extinct.

The seven most at-risk frogs are:

- The southern corroboree frog
- The northern corroboree frog
- The Baw Baw frog
- The spotted tree frog
- The Tasmanian tree frog
- The Kroombit tinker frog
- The armoured mist frog

CORROBOREE FROGS

There are two species of corroboree frog – the northern and southern corroboree frog. One species is Endangered and the other Critically Endangered. They are small, brightly coloured, ground-dwelling frogs that secrete a toxin poisonous to predators.

BAW BAW FROG

An infectious disease called chytrid fungus has decimated the population of this small, brown frog. Found only on the Mt Baw Baw plateau in Victoria, the Baw Baw frog lives underground and feeds on worms and other invertebrates.

KROOMBIT TINKER FROG

The Kroombit tinker frog is only found where water drains or under rocks in high altitude rainforests within the Kroombit Tops National Park and Kroombit Forest Reserve. The tinker frog is small, eats insects and makes a tinkering noise during mating season.

Main Threats to Frogs:

- Loss of wetland areas and damage to breeding sites
- The conversion of ponds and waterholes to dams for stock use. This results in cattle destroying the habitat
- Fungus and disease
- The forestry industry
- Tourism
- Pollution
- Climate change
- Chemicals and insecticides from agriculture polluting water
- Introduction of fish that prey on frog eggs and tadpoles
- Other predators
- Most frogs are salt intolerant, so a major issue is increased salinity

BACK FROM THE DEAD

In March 2013, a team from the University of New South Wales announced they had succeeded in growing early-stage cloned embryos containing the DNA of the gastric-brooding frog, which became extinct in 1983. No embryo survived, but the research continues in the hope to bring the frog back from extinction.

VULNERABLE CRAYFISH

Australia has about 135 species of freshwater crayfish, with more being regularly described. Crayfish are good indicators of water condition and monitoring them provides information on environmental issues such as salinity and altered currents within freshwater habitats.

The **FITZROY FALLS SPINY CRAYFISH** is found only in Wildes Meadow Creek on the New South Wales Southern highlands. Threats include habitat destruction and feral animals. A major threat is the common yabby which although native to Australia, has been introduced into the Falls spiny crayfish's environment. The Falls spiny crayfish creates burrows under the water in the stream bed. It has adapted to flowing stream conditions. The Fitzroy Falls Reservoir has altered its habitat by forming a large static body of water. The introduced yabby thrives in these conditions and feed on the spiny crayfish.

The **LECKIE'S CRAYFISH** is a small crayfish with a highly restricted distribution, making it particularly vulnerable and listed as Critically Endangered on the ICUN Red List. This crayfish has never been found outside of one small area of national park in Northern New South Wales. The invasion of feral species to this area, such as pigs and cane toads would severely impact the crayfish, as would any degradation to its habitat.

The **MURRAY CRAYFISH** is the second largest freshwater crayfish in the world. They live in parts of the Murray River and the Murrumbidgee River and in some dams. The female crayfish lays 500 to 1,000 eggs once a year and carries them under her tail as both eggs and when they hatch. They are long living and can live for up to 50 years. Major threats include changes to their habitat, especially water flow when dams and weirs are built.

ADD 3 MORE TO THAT LIST:

- Mallacoota burrowing crayfish
- Warragul burrowing crayfish
- Denison rain crayfish

CRITICALLY ENDANGERED

ENDANGERED SPECIES AREA

The Australian Fritillary

Australia has over 420 different species of butterfly but not all of them are indigenous. Around 230 butterfly species, or more than 60 per cent of Australia's butterflies, live in the World Heritage Rainforests of North Queensland. Many rely on freshwater environments such as wetlands for survival.

Butterflies perform an important environmental service by pollinating plants. Many butterflies are considered vulnerable, endangered and critically endangered mostly because of their highly specific habitats and reproductive habits. Butterfly conservation occurs on a state-to-state basis, with pressure for more to be done to save Australia's butterflies.

The Australian fritillary (also called laced fritillary) is listed as Critically Endangered. Their habitat has been restricted to the swampy coastal heathlands of the coast, where it feeds on the purple flower Viola betonicifolia.

Due to habitat loss, it is not just rare, but might already be extinct. The last specimen was collected near Port Macquarie in northern New South Wales in April 2001, with an additional sighting from Bribie Island in southeast Queensland around the same time. Anyone who spots an Australian fritillary is asked to make careful observations and try to photograph it and immediately contact the NSW Office of Environment and Heritage.

The Glenelg Freshwater Mussel

Some endangered species might not be as well-known as others. The Glenelg freshwater mussel is critically endangered, found only in streams in Victoria, Tasmania and South Australia.

Western Swamp Tortoise

NYOONGAR ABORIGINAL NAME: Yarkiny

One of Australia's most endangered reptiles, the western swamp tortoise is now restricted to only two small populations in the wild, numbering less than 200 in total. The tortoises are found near Perth in Western Australia, in swamps that fill in winter and spring. These small tortoises have a brown or black shell, short neck and webbed toes. They are carnivores and eat small invertebrates.

Main Threats:

- Their habitat has been modified or destroyed due to land clearing for agriculture and housing
- Changes in fire regimes
- The use of pesticides and fertilisers
- Climate change impacts their swamp habitats
- Predators such as cats and foxes eat their eggs

Saving the Western Swamp Tortoise

Perth Zoo has a program to save the Western Swamp Tortoise. Since 1989 the zoo has bred more than 800 tortoises of which 600 have been released back into the wild.

BIRDS UNDER THREAT

Australia is home to a wide range of birds, both endemic and migratory. There are 828 species of Australian native birds and nearly half are endemic. More than 80 per cent of Australia's parrots are found only in Australia and the country also boasts the highest diversity of honeyeaters in the world.

Since colonisation, nine bird species have become extinct. A further 50 are under threat or endangered. Millions of birds are killed each year as a result of deforestation and loss of habitat. Feral cats kill over one million birds a day, or 377 million birds annually.

Magpie Goose

The magpie goose is a large black and white bird found in wetlands. It has a black head, neck and wing tips. The underparts are white and it has a knob on the crown. They feed on grasses, bulbs and rhizomes. While magpie geese are widespread in northern Australia, they have disappeared from south eastern Australia. The magpie goose is listed Endangered in South Australia and Victoria and Vulnerable in New South Wales. The main threats are changes to and loss of habitat and predators eating their eggs and goslings.

The Powerful Owl

The powerful owl is the largest of Australia's owls and endemic to eastern and southeastern Australia's forests and woodlands. It inhabits a range of vegetation types, including wet forest and rainforest. They are carnivorous, eating small marsupials and rabbits. The powerful owl mates for life, sometimes for over 30 years. They are listed as Vulnerable in New South Wales and Endangered in Victoria. Their main threats are due to clearing of its habitat, including hollow trees.

Little Tern

Although secure at Federal level, the little tern is listed as Vulnerable or Endangered in a number of states. This white or grey bird has a black crown on its head. It feeds on insects, small fish, crustaceans and other invertebrates in its coastal habitats of beaches, rivers, estuaries and sheltered inlets. Coastal development has severely impacted the little tern's nesting sites.

BIRD'S NEST WITH EGGS LITTLE TERNS ON SAND

EXTINCT IN THE WILD

Pedder Galaxias

The Pedder galaxias is Australia's most endangered freshwater fish, and was recently very close to extinction. It is listed as Endangered under both the State and Federal Species Protection Acts.

The Pedder galaxias has a long slender, scaleless body and flat head. It is greenish brown, and sometimes even gold, with a dark, blotchy pattern. Its underbelly is lighter. They can grow to 160 millimetres, but are generally smaller than that and live for five to six years of age. They feed on insects and aquatic crustaceans.

It was endemic to Lake Pedder in southwestern Tasmania, but the lake was flooded in 1972 for hydro-electric power generation, which meant its habitat was completely altered. Then the introduction of trout into the lake nearly wiped the smaller Pedder galaxias out.

WHAT IS BEING DONE TO SAVE THE PEDDER GALAXIAS?

A program to ensure its survival began began in the early 1990s where about 50 of them were moved from Lake Pedder to Lake Oberon, or to a captive breeding program at Salmon Ponds. Today the species is thriving in Lake Oberon, with another backup population that was released at Strathgordon Water Supply Dam.

WHAT IS BEING DONE TO SAVE AUSTRALIA'S ENDANGERED SPECIES?

The Department of the Environment and Heritage administers *Australia's Endangered Species Protection Act*. Recovery projects study and conserve threatened species and their habitats, including plants, reptiles, amphibians, invertebrates, fish, mammals and birds.

Every state and territory has a conservation agency, which is involved in looking after habitats and management of species, including threatened species.

Organisations such as botanic gardens, zoos and universities are funded by state and federal governments to look after and research endangered animals. Some are trying to breed threatened species.

The Australian Government has established a new national approach to threatened species, which includes:

- tackling feral cats
- establishing safe havens for species most at risk
- emergency interventions to avert extinctions

Most endangered animals have a recovery plan to ensure the species' survival.

Feral Cats
The government is currently testing new baiting methods for feral cats with the aim of culling up to 2 million of them. Animal rights groups oppose this as barbaric.

WHAT CAN YOU DO ?

- Never dump a pet in the wild. They can survive and wreak havoc with native species. Take unwanted pets to the RSPCA.
- If you have a cat, attach a bell to its collar. Make sure it does not catch native birds or other animals.
- When fishing, don't lose any fishing line or hooks.
- Use less energy and use green energy where possible. The more sustainable your life is, the less you are contributing to climate change.
- Cut back on chemical use. Household, garden and agricultural chemicals end up in our river systems and ultimately the ocean.
- Turtle hatchlings use light and reflections from the moon to find their way to the water at night. Artificial lighting confuses them, so turn off lights visible from nesting beaches.
- Never litter. Pick up any rubbish you see on the beach. Cut back on plastic use, including plastic bags, straws and balloons.
- Never buy products that have been made from endangered animal parts.

Some Organisations That Provide More Information

The Foundation for Australia's Most Endangered Species (FAME)
https://www.fame.org.au/projects

Australian Wildlife Conservancy
http://www.australianwildlife.org

WWF Australia
http://www.wwf.org.au

URBAN HABITATS AND PIT STOPS

You can create places in your garden at home for animals to rest and find sanctuary.
Ways to do this include:

- adding plants that provide food to your garden.
- adding a water feature for birds or frogs.
- providing shelter, such as rocks for reptiles or nest boxes for birds.

SEARCH KEY WORDS

extinct, endangered, threatened species, riparian, vulnerable species, habitats, conservation, ecosystem, sustainability, salinity, Murray-Darling Basin, biodiversity

SOURCES

http://www.environment.gov.au
http://www.iucnredlist.org
http://www.wetlandcare.com.au
http://www.australianwildlife.org
https://www2.griffith.edu.au/australian-rivers-institute

Glossary

aquatic: related to water
catchment: an area of land which rainwater drains into a lake, river or stream
critical: at a turning point for survival
ecosystem: the living and non-living parts of an area
endangered: may soon become extinct
endemic: only found in a certain place
estuary: body of water where a river meets the sea
extinct: no longer in existence
feral predators: non-native animals that kill and eat other animals
habitat: place where plants and animals live
recovery plan: a plan for the conservation of a species
riparian: the land in the immediate vicinity of bodies of water, such as a river bank
salinity: damaging levels of salt on the land or in freshwater environments
silt: very fine soil
species: one kind of living thing
threat: anything that may reduce the numbers of a species
threatened: endangered or vulnerable
tropical: warm year round
vulnerable: may soon become endangered
wetlands: areas of land that are temporarily or permanently covered in water

Index

JOIN THE CELEBRATION

Australia celebrates National Threatened Species Day annually on **7 September.**